LSU

TIGERS

BY RAY FRAGER

Published by ABDO Publishing Company, PO Box 398166, Minneapolis, MN 55439. Copyright © 2013 by Abdo Consulting Group, Inc. International copyrights reserved in all countries. No part of this book may be reproduced in any form without written permission from the publisher. SportsZone™ is a trademark and logo of ABDO Publishing Company.

Printed in the United States of America,
North Mankato, Minnesota
052012
092012

Editor: Chrös McDougall
Series Designer: Craig Hinton

Photo Credits: Aaron M. Sprecher/AP Images, cover; Louisiana State/Collegiate Images/Getty Images, 1; Rogelio V. Solis/AP Images, 4, 7, 43 (bottom); Charlie Riedel/AP Images, 9; LSU/Collegiate Images/Getty Images, 10, 42 (top); AP Images, 14, 17, 18, 20, 23, 26, 28, 30, 42 (bottom left), 43 (top left); Jacob Harris/AP Images, 25, 43 (top right); Allsport/Getty Images, 33, 42 (bottom right); John Russell/AP Images, 34; Stephan Savioa/AP Images, 36; Dave Martin/AP Images, 39; Cal Sport Media via AP Images, 41; Hilary Scheinuk/LSU Sports Information/AP Images, 44

Library of Congress Cataloging-in-Publication Data
Frager, Ray.
  LSU Tigers / by Ray Frager.
    p. cm. -- (Inside college football)
  ISBN 978-1-61783-497-4
  1. Louisiana State University (Baton Rouge, La.)--Football--History--Juvenile literature. 2. LSU Tigers (Football team)--History--Juvenile literature. I. Title.
  GV958.L65F73 2011
  796.332'630976318--dc23
                        2012001850

TABLE OF CONTENTS

LSU quarterback Matt Flynn throws a
pass during the Tigers' 45–0 win over
Mississippi State in 2007.

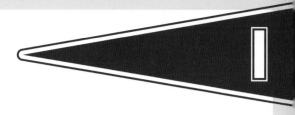

AN UNLIKELY CHAMPIONSHIP

THE FOOTBALL TEAM AT LOUISIANA STATE UNIVERSITY (LSU) NEEDED A LOT OF THINGS TO HAPPEN TO EARN A BERTH IN THE NATIONAL CHAMPIONSHIP GAME FOLLOWING THE 2007 SEASON. AND WHEN THOSE THINGS DID HAPPEN, THE TIGERS TOOK ADVANTAGE.

The 2007 season began on a high note. The Tigers began the season ranked second in the country. They started things off with a 45–0 shutout over Mississippi State. And they continued to win. By their sixth game, the Tigers were ranked number one in the nation. They held on to that ranking after beating number nine Florida 28–24.

But the Tigers stumbled in their next game, at Kentucky. After three overtimes, the seventeenth-ranked Wildcats came out on top, 43–37. One loss can sometimes end a team's chances for a national championship. But LSU came back to win its next two games. Both were against ranked

TIGERS

opponents. And by their eleventh game, the Tigers were back to number one in the country.

Then, in the final regular-season game, the Tigers hosted Arkansas. This game again required three overtime periods. And again, LSU came out on the wrong side, losing 50–48. The Tigers still won the Southeastern Conference (SEC) West division. But no team with two losses in a season had ever won the Bowl Championship Series (BCS) national championship. The BCS uses a series of polls and computers to determine the best teams in college football.

LSU went into the SEC Championship Game ranked fifth in the nation. The Tigers needed to be in the top two to be selected to the BCS National Championship Game. But then things happened just right for LSU.

It started with the Missouri Tigers. Missouri went into the Big 12 championship game ranked number one in the nation. Then it fell to ninth-ranked Oklahoma.

PICKING TALENT

Seven LSU players were selected in the 2008 National Football League (NFL) Draft. One of them, senior defensive tackle Glenn Dorsey, went fifth overall to the Kansas City Chiefs. Three more players went in the third round. They were senior cornerback Chevis Jackson, senior fullback Jacob Hester, and senior wide receiver Early Doucet. Senior safety Craig Steltz was picked in the fourth round, senior quarterback Matt Flynn went in the sixth round, and senior tight end Keith Zinger went in the seventh round.

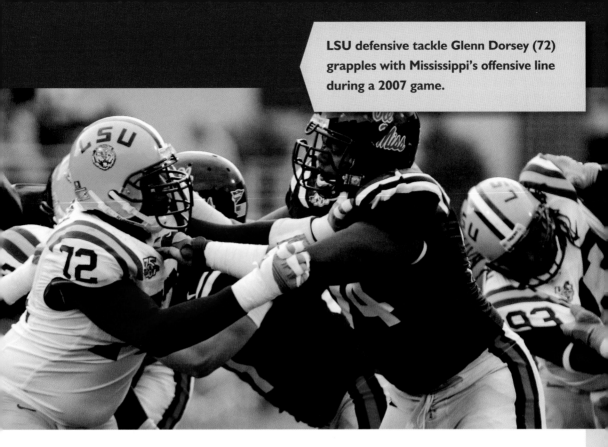

LSU defensive tackle Glenn Dorsey (72) grapples with Mississippi's offensive line during a 2007 game.

Next it was West Virginia's turn. The Mountaineers came into their regular-season-ending showdown with Pittsburgh ranked number two in the nation. A BCS title game berth appeared to be a done deal, as Pittsburgh had a losing record. But then West Virginia fell, too.

Even with those upsets at the top of the rankings, LSU still needed to win to have a shot at the national championship. And the Tigers would have to face Tennessee in the SEC title game with a backup quarterback. With senior starter Matt Flynn injured, sophomore backup Ryan Perrilloux took over. The Tigers scored just 21 points in the game. It was the least they had scored all year. But it was enough to hold off Tennessee, which only scored 14 points. And with the win, LSU jumped from seventh to second in the BCS rankings.

FROM STEEL TO SIDELINES

After graduating from the University of Michigan, Les Miles got into delivering steel in trucks. But that only lasted for a couple of years. Miles's mother, Martha Miles, said: "Oh, he worked hard at that. He tried. But he'd watch his younger brother Eric play football, and then finally he said to me one night, 'Mom, I really want to be a coach.'"

So Miles left the trucking business and went back to Michigan. He worked as an assistant coach to the legendary Bo Schembechler. It was not easy to get that job. Miles had to call and call and call before Schembechler would even get back to him. It took more than 30 calls. "He liked everything about Bo, his integrity, the way he worked, the way he knew his players," Martha Miles said. "He just absolutely worshipped Bo."

"By the grace of God we got here," Tigers coach Les Miles said. "Once we got here, we were going to do our best."

The Tigers still had to deal with some adversity as they waited to play Ohio State for the national title. Rumors circulated that Miles was going to leave LSU to take the head coaching job at Michigan. The job was open, and Miles had gone to college at Michigan. It was an emotional time for Miles and his players. In fact, Miles even started to cry in November while discussing the opening at Michigan with reporters.

The rumors had ended by January 7, 2008, when the Tigers played the Buckeyes for the national championship. That is because Michigan had hired someone else to be its head coach. So that just left Miles and the Tigers the job of beating the Buckeyes.

Ohio State jumped out to a 10–0 lead. But LSU worked its way back. The Tigers scored 31 consecutive points. Flynn threw four touchdown passes in the game. Senior defensive

back Chevis Jackson also played a major role. He batted away a sure touchdown pass when the game was still tied in the first half. Shortly thereafter, when LSU had only a seven-point lead, Jackson intercepted a pass to set up the second-quarter touchdown that put the Tigers ahead 24–10.

The Buckeyes helped by committing a load of penalties. In the end, for an LSU team that had played in six games decided by seven points or less, there was no nervous finish. The Tigers won 38–24.

"We knew we had the opportunity to come out here and make history," senior defensive end Kirston Pittman said. "We're the first team to win two BCS championships. We're the winningest [senior] class in LSU history."

AN UNLIKELY CHAMPIONSHIP

Doc Fenton became a star quarterback for LSU after moving from end to quarterback in 1908.

2

TO THE SUGAR BOWL AND BEYOND

THE FIRST-EVER COLLEGE FOOTBALL GAME WAS PLAYED IN 1869, BETWEEN RUTGERS AND PRINCETON. A LITTLE MORE THAN 20 YEARS LATER, LSU PLAYED ITS FIRST GAME. IN 1893, LSU FACED ANOTHER LOUISIANA SCHOOL CALLED TULANE. TULANE IS IN NEW ORLEANS, WHICH IS ABOUT 80 MILES (129 KM) FROM LSU'S BATON ROUGE CAMPUS. TODAY LSU IS A POWERHOUSE, WHILE TULANE PLAYS IN A SMALLER CONFERENCE. BUT THEIR FORTUNES WERE REVERSED IN THAT FIRST GAME, AS TULANE WON 34–0. THAT WAS THE ONLY GAME OF THE SEASON.

LSU had its first really successful football season in 1896. That year, the newly named Tigers went 6–0 under the direction of coach A. W. Jeardeau. That was also LSU's first season as a member of the Southern Intercollegiate Athletic Association (SIAA). The conference included other universities that would go on to become regular opponents for LSU. They included Alabama, Auburn, Georgia, Mississippi, and Tennessee.

MAKING HISTORY IN CUBA

On Christmas Day in 1907, LSU became the first college football team to play a game in another country. It played in Havana, Cuba. The game became known as the Bacardi Bowl. The Tigers took on the University of Havana. Havana's football team had beaten up on teams from the US military.

The LSU players were undersized compared to their Cuban opponents. But the Tigers' superior ball skills and elusive running were too much for the Havana team.

LSU shut out Havana 56–0. This delighted the large number of US military men in attendance at the game.

The star of the day was LSU quarterback Doc Fenton. The Cubans had nicknamed him "El Rubio Vaselino" for his red hair and slippery moves on the field.

"The Tigers" is a common name for sports teams. However, the LSU Tigers actually have a basis in history. During the Civil War, military units in Louisiana were nicknamed "Tigers." In fact, the Washington Artillery of New Orleans even used a tiger head as its symbol. So it made sense for LSU's sports teams to be named the Tigers.

Football in its early years hardly resembled today's game. The action on the field looked more like rugby than modern football. There was no television coverage, and stadiums were much smaller. Even the schedules back then could be inconsistent. For the next decade, LSU's schedule varied from as few as one game to as many as nine games per season. But in 1908, LSU had its initial great season by modern standards. The Tigers went undefeated in 10 games.

The star of that team was Doc Fenton. Tigers coach Edgar Wingard recruited Fenton from Scranton,

Pennsylvania. "I guess you could say I was among the first of the boys from coal country to come down to play football," Fenton said.

Fenton was the quarterback on the 1908 team. He switched to that position from end. Fenton was not happy about making the change. However, Wingard helped encourage him by giving him $70 to buy some clothes in downtown Baton Rouge. That might have been against college rules—even back then.

The undefeated Tigers were known for the skillful way they tossed the ball around on laterals. They sometimes used two or three laterals on a single play. As for Fenton, he was handy at tossing the ball, and he was a hard-to-catch runner. One of LSU's presidents, General Troy Middleton, said Fenton compared well with Jim Thorpe. Many consider Thorpe to be the greatest football player in the first half of the twentieth century. "I saw Jim Thorpe play," Middleton said, "but Doc [Fenton] was better."

After the 10–0 season, the next big event in LSU football history was in 1924. That is when the school opened Tiger Stadium. It remains the Tigers' home today. LSU's first game at Tiger Stadium was against Tulane in the last game of the 1924 season. The original stadium had room for 12,000 fans. However, additions were completed in 1931, 1936, 1953, and 1978. In 2012, Tiger Stadium could hold more than 92,000 people.

The SIAA had become the Southern Conference in the early 1920s. It had as many as 23 schools. But before the 1933 football season, 13 members of the Southern Conference—including LSU—broke away.

TO THE SUGAR BOWL AND BEYOND

All-American Gus Tinsley, shown in 1935, starred for LSU both as a pass rusher and a pass catcher.

They formed the SEC. Some original members have left and others have joined. However, the SEC has always contained LSU's biggest football rivals: Alabama, Auburn, Florida, Georgia, and Mississippi.

On January 1, 1935, New Orleans began to host a postseason football game called the Sugar Bowl. It remains one of the most

prestigious bowl games. LSU was not invited to the first Sugar Bowl, but the Tigers went to the next three. And even though LSU lost each time, it was the beginning of a successful run under coach Bernie Moore.

All-American end Gus Tinsley led Moore's first Sugar Bowl teams. In those days, players were used on both offense and defense. Tinsley was a valuable pass catcher and pass rusher. Moore said of him: "Tinsley could have made All-American at any position. He was so tough, he made blockers quit. He's the greatest lineman I ever saw."

LSU had played Texas Christian University (TCU) in its first Sugar Bowl game after the 1935 season. Tinsley chased after TCU's All-American quarterback, Sammy Baugh. With the scoring kept to a minimum because of muddy conditions, TCU beat LSU 3–2. The Tigers' only points came when Tinsley forced Baugh into a safety while Baugh was trying to pass. Had LSU beaten TCU, the Tigers might have been named national champions.

A FOOTBALL HERO AND A WAR HERO

Ken Kavanaugh became an All-American end for LSU in 1939, catching 30 passes. That might not sound like a lot today, but teams did not throw the ball very often during that time. After LSU, Kavanaugh had a long career as a player, coach, and scout in the NFL. However, he put his NFL life on hold to serve in the military during World War II. As a bomber pilot, he won two medals for his bravery in combat.

TO THE SUGAR BOWL AND BEYOND

GIVE HIM THE BALL!

Steve Van Buren became one of the NFL's all-time-great running backs and a member of the Pro Football Hall of Fame. But he barely got to carry the ball until his last season at LSU, in 1943. "He probably was the greatest running back in Southeastern Conference history," coach Bernie Moore said, "and I used him as a blocking back until his last year. The folks in Baton Rouge never let me forget that." Given a chance at running back as a senior, Van Buren led the nation in scoring with 98 points and ranked second in rushing yardage with 847.

In 1935, LSU finished the regular season ranked second in the country. But the Tigers again fell in the Sugar Bowl. This time Santa Clara won 21–14. LSU lost to Santa Clara in the Sugar Bowl the next season, too, falling 6–0.

After the Sugar Bowl following the 1937 season, LSU did not make it to a bowl game until 1943. Still, coach Moore kept the Tigers winning. They had only two losing records during his 13 seasons. Finally, the Tigers were invited to the Orange Bowl after the 1943 season. The Orange Bowl is another major bowl game.

Moore then took the Tigers to the Cotton Bowl after they went 9–1 in 1946. That Cotton Bowl was another postseason game that the Tigers had to play in miserable conditions. This time it was ice, sleet, and snow. LSU featured sophomore Y. A. Tittle at quarterback. He would go on to a Pro Football Hall of Fame career. However, LSU could not score against Arkansas, and the game ended in a 0–0 tie.

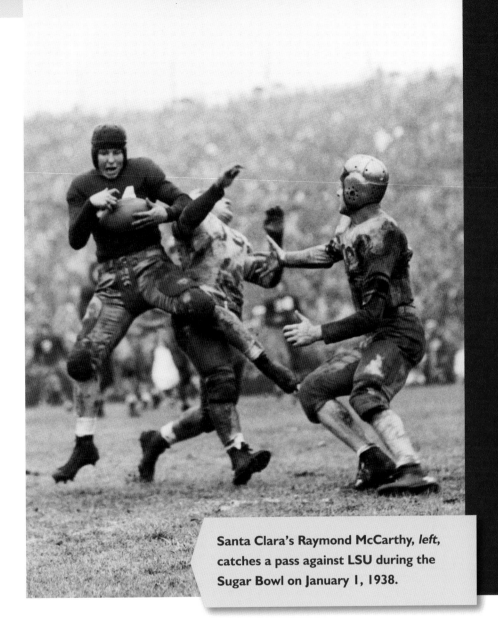

Santa Clara's Raymond McCarthy, *left*, catches a pass against LSU during the Sugar Bowl on January 1, 1938.

Moore coached one more season. Then his former player, Tinsley, replaced him as head coach in 1948. Fans hoped he was as good a coach as he was as a player.

Former LSU star Gus Tinsley returned to coach the Tigers in 1948.

3

MARCHING TO A TITLE

FORMER LSU STAR GUS TINSLEY TOOK OVER AS THE TIGERS' COACH IN 1948. IN 1949, TINSLEY DIRECTED LSU BACK TO THE SUGAR BOWL AFTER POSTING AN 8–1 REGULAR SEASON RECORD. BUT OKLAHOMA POUNDED THE TIGERS 35–0 IN THE BOWL GAME, AND THAT WAS THE LAST BOWL GAME FOR LSU UNDER TINSLEY. THE TIGERS HAD LOSING RECORDS IN THREE OF THE NEXT FIVE SEASONS.

Tinsley's last season was 1954. His Tigers featured All-American senior tackle Sid Fournet. He played both offense and defense. And in 1954, Fournet was on the field for 83 percent of the Tigers' plays.

But LSU needed a change of coach. In 1955, Paul Dietzel became the man in charge. He arrived in Baton Rouge after serving as an assistant coach at Army. Dietzel had prepared for his first head coaching job by working under and alongside some of the greatest coaches of all time. Among them were Red Blaik, Bear Bryant, Vince Lombardi, and Sid Gillman.

At age 31, he was the youngest head coach in the country when he began in 1955.

"LSU invited me down to be interviewed," Dietzel said, "and I came down not knowing much about LSU at that time."

Dietzel installed a unique system of rotating players in and out of the game. The White Team was the starters on offense and defense. The Go Team was the second-string group on offense. And the Chinese Bandits were the second group on defense.

CHINESE BANDITS

How did coach Paul Dietzel come up with the name "Chinese Bandits" for his second-team defense? It originated from a comic strip called Terry and the Pirates. A character in the comic said Chinese bandits were "the most vicious people on Earth." That was the kind of toughness Dietzel wanted from his players.

In his first three seasons, Dietzel had records of 3–5–2, 3–7, and 5–5. The best player for LSU during that time was fullback Jim Taylor. He became better known for his role with the NFL's Green Bay Packers. But Taylor first showed off his bruising running style for the Tigers. He would try to run directly into a would-be tackler rather than around him.

"I tried to initiate the contact," Taylor said. "That might be a little bit different than the normal running back. . . . If you drop down and initiate the contact with that cornerback or linebacker, I might pick up another 18 inches—which may make the difference in measuring for a first down."

Taylor led the SEC in rushing yards in his junior and senior seasons, 1956 and 1957. The team only kept improving in 1958. That year, the Tigers ran through their entire schedule without a loss. They finished off an 11–0 season with a Sugar Bowl victory and the school's first national championship.

Junior running back Billy Cannon led the Tigers. He possessed a combination of speed and strength that made him unique in college

FIGHTING OVER CANNON

Professional football was just beginning to truly take off in 1959, when Heisman Trophy winner Billy Cannon played his final year at LSU. The American Football League (AFL) was created in 1960 to challenge the established NFL. One of the ways the AFL and NFL fought each other was over players. Both leagues wanted Cannon. He actually signed contracts with teams from the AFL and the NFL.

"You know when people come up to you and put money, cash money, you take it and put it into your pocket," he said.

The matter of the two contracts ended up in court, and Cannon ended up going to the Houston Oilers of the AFL. He also played for the Oakland Raiders and the Kansas City Chiefs during his 11 years in professional football. After starting out as a running back in college, Cannon switched to tight end with the Raiders.

football. "Billy's by far the best athlete I've ever coached," Dietzel said. "He's stronger, faster, tougher. He can do more things well. And he improves from week to week. Give him a step and he's gone. But if there's no room, he'll run over you. When he does it hurts." Cannon also played defense, did some of the kicking, and threw the occasional pass.

The Chinese Bandits defensive unit played a big role in the 1958 team, too. Those players were not as talented as the first-team players. But they made up for it with their high spirit. In fact, players who were promoted to the White Team would often want to stay as members of the Chinese Bandits. "They are the darnedest bunch of kids you ever saw," Dietzel said.

The Bandits, with their swarming, gang-tackling style, helped LSU record four shutouts in that championship season. None of those shutouts were more important than the 14–0 victory

over Mississippi in the seventh game of the season. LSU had moved into the number-one spot in the national rankings the week before. The showdown drew the first sellout crowd to fill the 67,500 seats in Tiger Stadium. The key series came in the second quarter. Mississippi had five tries to score from LSU's 2-yard line, but the offense was unable to cross the goal line.

Back then, the final polls for college football actually came before bowl games. So the most respected polls all named LSU as the national champions before the Tigers' Sugar Bowl game against Clemson.

MARCHING TO A TITLE

But LSU did not let up in that bowl game. Cannon threw a touchdown pass for the game's only score. The Tigers defeated Clemson 7–0.

Cannon already had a place in the school's football history after leading the Tigers to their first national championship as a junior. But in his senior year, Cannon established himself as perhaps the greatest LSU football player ever.

On Halloween night in 1959, Cannon made what many consider the most famous play in LSU football history. LSU trailed rival Mississippi 3–0 in the fourth quarter. Then Cannon ran back a punt 89 yards for a touchdown. He showed off the qualities that made him such a terrific player. Cannon's strength allowed him to break several attempted tackles. Then his speed carried him to the end zone. His touchdown provided the margin of victory in a 7–3 win.

HE SAID IT

"That was the greatest run I ever saw in football." —LSU coach Paul Dietzel on Billy Cannon's 1959 punt return for a touchdown against Mississippi

LSU finished the 1959 season with another appearance in the Sugar Bowl. This time, the Tigers lost in a rematch with Mississippi. With a 9–2 record, the Tigers finished the season ranked third. Although they did not win another national championship, Cannon won that year's Heisman Trophy as the best player in college football.

Running back Billy Cannon became the first LSU player to win the Heisman Trophy in 1959.

Dietzel coached two more seasons at LSU. In his final year, he led the 1961 Tigers to a 10–1 record, an Orange Bowl berth, and a final ranking of number four. And the winning tradition would only grow with the next coach.

Charlie McClendon, LSU's all-time winningest coach, was inducted into the College Football Hall of Fame in 1986.

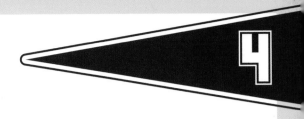

CONSISTENTLY GOOD

AFTER PAUL DIETZEL LEFT LSU, ONE OF HIS ASSISTANTS, CHARLIE MCCLENDON, GRABBED THE WHISTLE IN 1962. MCCLENDON SERVED AS HEAD COACH THROUGH 1979. IN THE PROCESS, HE BECAME LSU'S ALL-TIME WINNINGEST COACH WITH A 137–59–7 RECORD. THE BOWL APPEARANCES PILED UP (13), AS DID THE ALL-AMERICANS HE COACHED (17).

The star of McClendon's first team was senior halfback Jerry Stovall. He finished runner-up in the voting for the Heisman Trophy that year. But Stovall won plenty of other honors. He was named an All-American and selected as the Most Valuable Player in the SEC. A versatile player, Stovall caught plenty of passes, ran back kicks, punted, and played defensive back. In fact, it was as a defensive back that Stovall played nine years in the NFL.

Stovall and his teammates finished off McClendon's first season with a victory over previously undefeated Texas in the Cotton Bowl. That gave LSU a 9–1–1 record.

LSU was making a habit of playing in bowl games nearly every year. A return trip to the Cotton Bowl on New Year's Day in 1966 proved to be the most memorable. The opponent that year was another undefeated squad—Arkansas. McClendon decided to motivate his Tigers by having the players on the practice team wear red like Arkansas. But he went a step further than that, too.

"Arkansas had won 22 straight games, and for two weeks in our preparation we had red jerseys for our scout squad and all the numbers on them were 23," McClendon said. "We just said, 'Fellas, you are going

to be victim number 23 if they beat us.'
After a while, that irritated the guys
something awful."

LSU did not become number 23.
The Tigers defeated Arkansas 14–7.

The Tigers had another memorable
season five years later, in 1970.
McClendon coached the Tigers to
the SEC title, a 9–3 record, a spot in
the Orange Bowl, and the number
seven national ranking. For his efforts,
McClendon shared National Coach of
the Year honors with Texas' Darrell
Royal. McClendon's most-decorated
player was safety Tommy Casanova. He
was a three-time All-American from
1969 through 1971.

The United States had been
segregated for most of its history. Many
southern universities' football teams
remained all-white through the 1960s
and into the early 1970s. That changed
at LSU in 1973. Lora Hinton became the
Tigers' first African-American player and
the first African American to be awarded a football scholarship.

MAKING THE MOST OF HIS TIME

Bert Jones did not become a starting quarterback at LSU until the very end of his junior season. Still, he made a big impact during his senior year in 1972. Jones, a native of Ruston, Louisiana, finished fourth in voting for the Heisman Trophy and was named to several All-America teams. Jones's biggest play at LSU came against rival Mississippi. His touchdown pass on the last play of the game gave the Tigers a 17–16 victory.

The Baltimore Colts selected Jones with the second pick in the NFL Draft, and he had a stellar professional career. Even before entering the NFL, Jones's strong arm had earned him the nickname "The Ruston Rifle." In fact, football observers often rank Jones as having one of the strongest throwing arms in the history of the NFL.

CONSISTENTLY GOOD

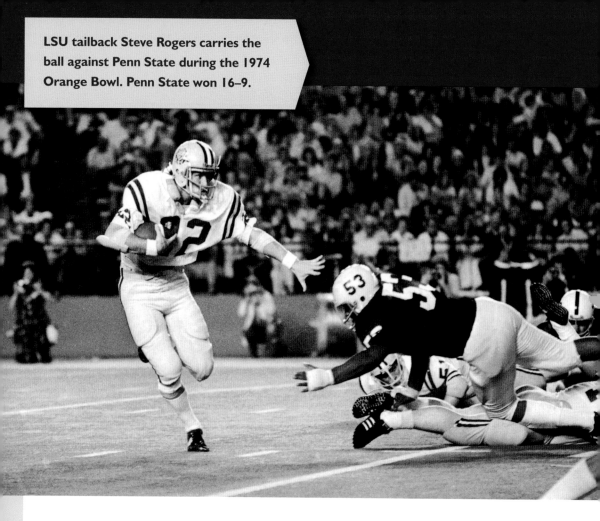

LSU tailback Steve Rogers carries the ball against Penn State during the 1974 Orange Bowl. Penn State won 16–9.

Hinton said some areas around the LSU campus still did not want to admit blacks, but his teammates would not allow him to be excluded. "When the team went there, they made sure that I was there, and if anybody had any problem with that, they had to deal with those guys. That's just the way it was," Hinton said.

McClendon continued to guide winning teams and earn bowl berths. However, he eventually was forced to resign after the 1979 season. That was because his success at LSU did not extend to beating SEC power Alabama. Bear Bryant, who had been McClendon's coach at Kentucky,

ALEXANDER THE GREAT

The best LSU running back after Billy Cannon was Charles Alexander. He rushed for more than 1,000 yards in his junior and senior seasons and set 27 LSU records by the end of his senior season in 1978. In a 1977 game against Oregon, Alexander ran for 237 yards and scored four touchdowns. He went on to the NFL and played in a Super Bowl with the Cincinnati Bengals. "Make sure to capitalize the 'G' on 'Great,' because that's exactly what he was for us," LSU coach Charlie McClendon said.

led Alabama. And McClendon went just 2–14 against the Crimson Tide. "That was a sore spot with a lot of people," McClendon said. "But there weren't many people beating Bear in those days."

Bo Rein was named as McClendon's replacement for 1980, but he never coached a game. Rein died in an airplane accident in January 1980. Former LSU star Jerry Stovall then became head coach.

Stovall lasted just four seasons. His 1982 team achieved a number 11 ranking and went to the Orange Bowl. But LSU had two losing records in those four years. When the Tigers finished 4–7 in 1983, not even Stovall's popularity in Louisiana could save his job.

The next five years were better for LSU. Under two coaches, the Tigers won at least eight games each season and went to a bowl game every year.

Bill Arnsparger replaced Stovall. The veteran coach got the Tigers to the Sugar Bowl after the 1984 and 1986 seasons. They also won the SEC

CONSISTENTLY GOOD

championship in 1986. Before coming to LSU, Arnsparger had coached for 20 years in the NFL, including two and a half years as head coach of the New York Giants. After three seasons at LSU, he retired from coaching and became the athletic director at Florida.

Several great players played under Arnsparger. Among them were linebacker Michael Brooks, wide receiver Wendell Davis, running back Dalton Hilliard, and quarterback Tommy Hodson. But Arnsparger did leave LSU with a bowl-game losing streak. The Tigers lost in each of the three postseason games they played under him.

Mike Archer, one of Arnsparger's top assistants, replaced him as head coach. Archer turned in a terrific first season in 1987. The Tigers went 10–1–1 and won the Gator Bowl. Their number five final ranking was LSU's highest since 1961. In the Gator Bowl, both Hodson and Davis had big games in a 30–13 victory over South Carolina. Hodson completed 20 of 32 passes. And Davis caught nine passes for 132 yards and three touchdowns.

LSU shared the SEC championship the next season and went to another bowl game. But 1988 was the last winning season for a while. The next year, LSU began a string of six consecutive losing records. Archer was gone after 1990. His replacement, Curley Hallman, made it through four years before also being fired.

In 1995, Gerry DiNardo got LSU back on a winning track. The Tigers reached three straight bowl games and returned to the national rankings. DiNardo's first teams featured explosive running back Kevin

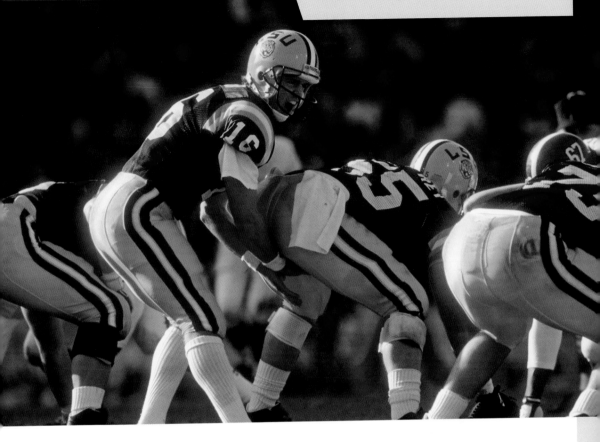

Faulk and a solid blocker in guard Alan Faneca. Both went on to make big impacts in the NFL.

However, DiNardo closed out the 1990s with two losing seasons. He was gone after five years in Baton Rouge. But as the 2000s began, LSU was about to start its greatest decade of football.

CONSISTENTLY GOOD

[33]

LSU running back Domanick Davis leaps over a Tennessee player during a kick return in a 2001 game.

AMONG THE ELITE

THE TIGERS HAD EXPERIENCED SUCCESS THROUGHOUT THEIR FIRST CENTURY. BUT THEY WERE NEVER AS CONSISTENTLY EXCELLENT AS THEY WERE FROM 2000 THROUGH 2011. THEY NEVER WON FEWER THAN EIGHT GAMES IN A SEASON IN THAT TIME. THEY WENT TO A BOWL GAME EVERY YEAR. AND THEY FINISHED RANKED IN THE TOP 10 SEVEN TIMES. LSU HAD BECOME ONE OF COLLEGE FOOTBALL'S PERENNIAL POWERS.

It started slowly. After the 1999 season, LSU hired Nick Saban as coach. He had a long coaching career before that. Saban's first assistant coaching job was in 1973. He worked for seven colleges and two NFL teams. He was Michigan State's head coach for five years before coming to LSU.

Saban's first LSU team went 8–4, played in the Peach Bowl, and ended up ranked number 22. He made a bigger splash the next year. The Tigers finished 10–3 and earned a berth in the Sugar Bowl. After beating Illinois in the Sugar Bowl, they ended the season ranked seventh.

The 2001 squad had a high-powered offense. The Tigers scored at least 30 points in eight games. The passing combination of senior quarterback Rohan Davey and junior wide receiver Josh Reed was especially good. Davey averaged nearly 280 yards passing per game. And Reed caught 94 passes for 1,740 yards during the season. In a November victory over Alabama, Reed set an LSU record with 19 catches.

LSU took a step back the next year, finishing 8–5 and out of the top 25 after the season. The Tigers did not seem like a sure thing heading into the 2003 season. Junior quarterback Matt Mauck was coming off an injury in 2002. Game-changing linebacker Bradie James had graduated. And the top two running backs also had left college.

But LSU rolled through its first three games. The Tigers were ranked tenth in the nation going into their first big test, against seventh-ranked Georgia. LSU had not beaten Georgia in 13 years. In a tight game, LSU did not take the lead for good until a Mauck-to-Skyler Green touchdown pass with less than 1:30 left on the clock. The Tigers held on for the 17–10 victory. Two weeks later, though, Florida dealt LSU a 19–7 defeat. But that was to be the Tigers' only loss that season.

LSU ran through the rest of the regular season. It toppled its SEC competition—South Carolina, Auburn, Alabama, Mississippi, and Arkansas. That put the Tigers into an SEC Championship Game rematch with Georgia. The third-ranked Tigers dominated, pulling away to a 34–13 victory. The Tigers racked up 444 yards of offense to Georgia's 249.

The victory propelled LSU into the BCS National Championship Game. It was being played in a familiar bowl—the Sugar Bowl. LSU's opponent was Oklahoma.

THERE HE GOES . . .

One of the most exciting players to come out of LSU in the 2000s was cornerback Patrick Peterson. In his third and final season at LSU, he won the 2010 Jim Thorpe Award as the country's best defensive back. But it was his ability as a punt returner that really made fans notice him. In his rookie season with the NFL's Arizona Cardinals in 2011, he ran back four punts for touchdowns, including a 99-yarder.

AMONG THE ELITE

TIGERS

The Sooners featured Heisman Trophy-winning quarterback Jason White. But the Tigers were not intimidated. White completed only 13 of his 37 passes. He threw two interceptions and was sacked five times. Junior defensive end Marcus Spears returned one of those interceptions for a touchdown. That was enough to secure LSU's 21–14 win.

However, LSU had to share the second national championship in school history. The Tigers were winners of the BCS title. But the University of Southern California ended up number one in the Associated Press Poll.

The next season, LSU could not maintain such heights. The Tigers dropped to 9–3 and a final number 16 ranking. And they lost their coach. Saban left after LSU completed its 2004 season with a loss in the Capital One Bowl. He took over as coach of the NFL's Miami Dolphins.

The new man in charge was Les Miles. He had been head coach at Oklahoma State for the previous four seasons. At Oklahoma State, he took a team that had been down and helped it rise. The Cowboys had

FAST START, SLOW FINISH

Justin Vincent got off to a terrific start in his college football career. As a freshman running back at LSU, he gained 1,001 yards and scored 10 touchdowns during the national championship season of 2003. But he was unable to match that season in his last three years. He gained approximately another 1,000 yards combined. No NFL team drafted Vincent. Though he made professional practice squads, he did not get to carry the ball in any NFL games.

only one bowl appearance in 12 seasons before Miles took over. Then Miles took them to three bowl games in a row.

If there were any questions about Miles's hire, he answered them quickly. Giant sophomore quarterback JaMarcus Russell led LSU to an 11–2 record and to the Peach Bowl in 2005. The Tigers finished the season ranked fifth overall. That was followed by another 11–2 record in 2006, along with a Sugar Bowl spot, and a number three ranking. Then came LSU's third national championship season in 2007.

Though the Tigers did not make the top 25 in the final 2008 rankings, it was but a temporary setback. In 2009 and 2010, they won

AMONG THE ELITE

JAMARCUS RUSSELL

JaMarcus Russell was LSU's starting quarterback the first two years that Les Miles was the Tigers' head coach. He seemed to be headed for professional stardom after leaving college. Russell was 6 feet 6 inches and 260 pounds. That body type was more similar to the linemen blocking for him and trying to sack him than to other quarterbacks. So he could withstand defenders attacking him when he dropped back to pass and then unleash one of his hard throws.

The Oakland Raiders picked Russell first overall in the 2007 NFL Draft. But he never enjoyed success in the NFL. The Raiders went just 7–18 in games he started, and the team released him after three seasons. As a professional quarterback, Russell was overweight and it was said he did not work hard enough.

nine and eleven games, respectively, and rated among the nation's best teams.

Then the Tigers returned to the very top of the rankings in 2011. The fourth-ranked Tigers opened the season with a 40–27 win over third-ranked Oregon. The Ducks had been the national runners-up in 2010. LSU was ranked number one by its fifth game, and it held on to that ranking as it went undefeated through the regular season.

The biggest game was that November at Alabama. The Crimson Tide came into the game ranked number two. Saban had also since taken over as Alabama's coach. The game turned into a classic SEC-style defensive struggle. The teams were tied 6–6 after four quarters, but LSU finally won on a field goal in overtime. More than 100,000 people were in attendance for the game between the top-ranked teams.

LSU and Alabama were both in the SEC West. So only LSU went to

the SEC Championship Game. But they did meet in the BCS National Championship Game after LSU won the SEC. The game was in the heart of SEC country in New Orleans. And once again, defense dominated. Unfortunately for LSU, it was mostly Alabama's defense. The Crimson Tide won 21–0, and the Tigers finished the season ranked number two.

It was a disappointing ending for the Tigers. But the season again proved that LSU is a football program whose rich history is seemingly matched only by its bright future.

AMONG THE ELITE

TIMELINE

LSU plays its first football game, losing to Tulane 34–0.

LSU joins the SIAA.

On Christmas Day, LSU becomes the first college football team to play a game outside of the United States, beating the University of Havana in Cuba.

LSU quarterback Doc Fenton leads the Tigers to a 10–0 season. The Tigers run a unique offense that uses lots of laterals.

Tiger Stadium opens.

| 1893 | 1896 | 1907 | 1908 | 1924 |

Charlie McClendon becomes LSU's head coach.

Lora Hinton becomes LSU's first African-American football player.

Star running back Charles Alexander finishes his LSU career with 27 school records.

One year after sharing the SEC title, LSU begins a streak of six consecutive losing seasons.

Nick Saban takes over as LSU's head coach and turns the Tigers into a contender.

| 1962 | 1973 | 1978 | 1989 | 2000 |

The SEC is formed, with LSU as a charter member.

On New Year's Day, LSU plays in its first Sugar Bowl, losing to TCU 3–2.

LSU goes 11–0 and wins its first national championship with help from the Chinese Bandits defensive unit.

On Halloween night, Billy Cannon runs 89 yards on a punt return for a touchdown in a victory over Mississippi. It is arguably the most famous play in LSU history.

Billy Cannon wins the Heisman Trophy. He remained LSU's only Heisman Trophy winner through 2011.

1933   **1936**   **1958**   **1959**   **1959**

LSU beats Oklahoma in the Sugar Bowl on January 4 to win the BCS national championship.

Les Miles takes over as the Tigers' head coach.

A perfect storm of events helps the 11–2 Tigers earn a berth in the BCS National Championship Game.

LSU defeats Ohio State in the BCS National Championship Game on January 7.

LSU reaches the BCS National Championship Game but falls to SEC rival Alabama.

2004   **2005**   **2007**   **2008**   **2011**

QUICK STATS

PROGRAM INFO
Louisiana State University Tigers (1893–)

NATIONAL CHAMPIONSHIPS
(* DENOTES SHARED TITLE)
1958, 2003*, 2007

OTHER ACHIEVEMENTS
BCS bowl appearances: (1999–): 5
SEC championships (1933–): 11
Bowl record: 22–20–1

HEISMAN TROPHY WINNERS
Billy Cannon, 1959

KEY PLAYERS
(POSITION[S]; SEASONS WITH TEAM)
Charles Alexander (RB; 1975–78)
Billy Cannon (HB, DB; 1957–59)
Warren Capone (LB; 1971–73)
Tommy Casanova (RB, DB; 1969–71)
Glenn Dorsey (DT; 2004–07)
Kevin Faulk (RB; 1995–98)
Bradie James (LB; 1999–2002)
Bert Jones (QB; 1970–72)
Josh Reed (WR; 1999–2001)
Jerry Stovall (RB, DB; 1960–62)

* All statistics through 2011 season

KEY COACHES
Paul Dietzel (1955–61):
    46–24–3; 2–1 (bowl games)
Charlie McClendon (1962–79):
    137–59–7; 7–6 (bowl games)
Les Miles (2005–):
    75–18; 5–2 (bowl games)

HOME STADIUM
Tiger Stadium (1924–)

"This team is full of grown men, guys who've been there before, guys who never quit. We just knew we had to keep going. We had a lot of time. We just had to keep moving along just like we've done all year." —Matt Flynn, quarterback of the 2007 national champion team

During LSU's 10–0 season in 1908, the Tigers defeated Auburn 10–2. Auburn's only points came on a safety, when it blocked a punt by LSU's star, Doc Fenton, in the end zone. Fenton said after the block that he was trying to pick up the bouncing ball when an Auburn fan interfered. The fans were right next to the field in the end zone, separated from the players by only a rope. "A fan reached over the rope and cracked me on the head with a cane," Fenton said. "It knocked me cold."

"With the ball under his arm, Jimmy Taylor was the best running back I've ever coached. He was just so versatile." —LSU coach Paul Dietzel

The first live Mike the Tiger mascot arrived on the LSU campus in 1936. He was bought from a zoo in Little Rock, Arkansas. The tiger was named Mike in honor of LSU's athletic director, Mike Chambers. He was the man behind the effort to get the tiger. The first Mike lived to be 20. Through 2011, there have been six Mikes at LSU.

GLOSSARY

adversity
Bad luck or obstacles that get in the way or cause problems. In sports, this refers to things that can keep a team from winning, such as injuries.

All-American
A player chosen as one of the best amateurs in the country in a particular activity.

athletic director
An administrator who oversees the coaches, players, and teams of an institution.

conference
In sports, a group of teams that plays each other each season.

draft
A system used by professional sports leagues to select new players in order to spread incoming talent among all teams. The NFL Draft is held each spring.

rival
An opponent that brings out great emotion in a team, its fans, and its players.

sack
In football, tackling the quarterback behind the line of scrimmage when he is trying to pass.

scholarship
Financial assistance awarded to students to help them pay for school. Top athletes earn scholarships to represent a college through its sports teams.

segregation
The practice of keeping people of different races separate from each other, often enforced by law.

stellar
Like a star. In sports, it refers to doing something great.

FOR MORE INFORMATION

FURTHER READING

Glier, Ray. *What It Means To Be A Tiger: Les Miles and LSU's Greatest Players*. Chicago: Triumph Books, 2009.

Rabalais, Scott. *The Fighting Tigers 1993–2008: Into a New Century of LSU Football*. Baton Rouge, LA: Louisiana State University Press, 2008.

Vincent, Herb. *LSU Football Vault: The History of the Fighting Tigers*. Atlanta, GA: Whitman Publishing, 2008.

WEB LINKS

To learn more about the LSU Tigers, visit ABDO Publishing Company online at **www.abdopublishing.com**. Web sites about the Tigers are featured on our Book Links page. These links are routinely monitored and updated to provide the most current information available.

PLACES TO VISIT

College Football Hall of Fame
111 South St. Joseph St.
South Bend, IN 46601
1-800-440-FAME (3263)
www.collegefootball.org

This hall of fame and museum highlights the greatest players and moments in the history of college football. Among the former Tigers enshrined here are Billy Cannon, Tommy Casanova, and Doc Fenton.

Tiger Stadium
North Stadium Drive
Baton Rogue, LA 70893
225-388-8226
www.lsusports.net/ViewArticle.dbml?DB_ OEM_ID=5200&ATCLID=177159

This has been LSU's home field since 1924. It holds 92,542 fans on Saturdays in the fall. Tours are available.

INDEX

ABOUT THE AUTHOR

Ray Frager is a freelance writer based in the Baltimore, Maryland area. He has been a professional sports editor and writer since 1980. He has worked for the *Trenton Times*, the *Dallas Morning News*, the *Baltimore Sun*, FOXSports.com, and Comcast SportsNet. At the *Sun*, he edited books on Cal Ripken Jr., the building of Baltimore's football stadium, and the Baltimore Ravens' 2000 Super Bowl season. He also has written several books about sports for kids.